Bundle of Joy

Kamakshi Jasra Sharma

BookLeaf Publishing

India | USA | UK

Presentation by *BookLeaf Publishing*

Web: www.bookleafpub.com

E-mail: info@bookleafpub.com

ISBN: 9789360944636

First edition 2024

DEDICATION

This book is lovingly dedicated to my own bundle of joy, who brings endless light and love into my days.

To God, for the countless blessings and the most wonderful experiences bestowed upon me, guiding my journey through both verse and life.

To my family, who have unearthed depths of me I never knew existed, nurturing and challenging me to grow beyond my imagined limits.

And to my friends, steadfast companions who have stood by my side through thick and thin, proving that loyalty and laughter are indeed life's invaluable treasures.

Together, you all reinforce my belief in the inherent goodness of life and inspire me to spread happiness wherever I go.

PREFACE

Welcome to *Bundle of Joy*, a heartfelt exploration of the positive spirits and serene beauty brought into our lives by animals, birds, and nature. This collection of poems is an ode to the countless ways in which the natural world uplifts, inspires, and enriches our existence.

Each poem in this book is a small window into the profound connections we share with the living tapestry around us. From the joyous chirping of birds at dawn to the loyal companionship of our pets, and the silent wisdom of ancient trees—these pages aim to capture the essence of what these experiences mean to us, and how they shape our perception of the world.

Bundle of Joy is more than just a book; it is an invitation to pause and notice the smaller joys that hide in plain sight. It is a call to celebrate the ordinary miracles like the warmth of a sunbeam, the resilience of a daisy on the sidewalk, or the steadfastness of the mountains. Through verse, we pay tribute to the natural world's role as a constant source of wonder and solace in our lives.

As you turn these pages, I hope you find moments of peace, a renewed sense of wonder, and a deeper appreciation for the little parcels of joy that life, in its generosity, bestows upon us daily. May these poems remind you of the beauty that surrounds us, waiting to be acknowledged, celebrated, and preserved.

Thank you for embarking on this journey through the beauty of the natural world, as seen through the eyes of joy and wonder. Enjoy the voyage.

Ever Grateful for Sunshine

Each morning brings her gentle grace,
A golden gleam upon my face.
My sunshine, small yet vast in light,
Illuminates the darkest night.

Her warmth, a constant guide to me,
In her rays, life's beauty I see.
She teaches me to grow and strive,
Under her glow, I come alive.

With every sunrise, hope is born,
Her light, the herald of the morn.
She spreads her joy, both far and wide,
In her embrace, I take my pride.

Her strength in me, steadfast, profound,
Where she is, my purpose is found.

She's more than light; she's life's sweet song,
Beside her bright, is where I belong.

Together, like the earth and sun,
A cosmic dance, forever spun.
My greatest strength, my heart's delight,
For she is day, and I, her light.

The Joyful Dolphin Leaps Across the Waves

Jubilantly bounding, a spectacle at sea
Over azure depths, in boundless glee
Yearning for the ocean's vast embrace
Free in its aquatic space
Under the waves, a dance so deft
Lifting spirits with each breath

The Inspired Eagle Reigns Over Mountain Skies

In lofty heights where silence dwells
Noble predator with a gaze that compels
Soaring above craggy peaks
Power in each stroke it seeks
In the vast heavens, a solitary figure
Reaching for dreams with vigorous vigor
Each flap imbues a majestic stride
Destined to conquer, with wings spread wide

A Dog's walk

Look at the Dog with lots of love to give,
Look at him smile and weave for miles.
With every wag, his joy spills over,
In fields of green and sweet clover.

His eyes, a spark of kindly light,
A beacon in the darkest night.
Each bound and leap, a verse of cheer,
His laughter rings, drawing near.

In parks and paths, he finds his stage,
Each sprint a line on life's bright page.
A friend to all, his heart so vast,
In his presence, shadows are cast.

Through simple games and gentle nuzzles,
He dissolves the world's big puzzles.
With a nudge, a lick, he shares his grace,
In every heart, he finds his place.

So look at the dog, with love so true,
A reminder of how joy can renew.
In every step, his love's unfurled,
A four-pawed joy, a better world.

A Grateful Dog Brings Joy and Loyalty

Greeting with barks filled with mirth
Resilient companion, unmatched in worth
Affectionate gaze, loyalty profound
Tail wagging, happiness unbound
Emotive eyes, tales untold
Faithful friend, pure as gold
Unwavering in joy they bring
Love incarnate, heart's offering

The Radiant Peacock Flaunts Its Majestic Plumes

Resplendent in a cloak of iridescent hues
Admired widely, a spectacle to peruse
Dazzling all with a vibrant display
Icon of beauty, nature's array
Artistry in each feathered span
Noble creature, pride of the land
Trails of color, nature's grace

Blooming Happiness in Delhi

In Delhi's heart, as winter wanes,
The gardens burst with joyful strains.
Pansies smile in playful hues,
Petunias spread in vibrant blues.

Dahlias stand with regal grace,
Commanding awe in their embrace.
But at their feet, a magic lies
Where petunias like carpets rise.

A quilt of colors soft and bright,
Under the clear and gentle light.
Pink whispers to the morning dew,
While purple sings a chorus true.

This spectacle revives the soul,
Filling the empty, making whole.
In every petal's gentle sway,
Delhi's February finds its way.

The air is crisp, the skies are clear,
And in this bloom, we hold dear
The joy that comes when flowers meet,
In the dance of life, vivid and sweet.

The Peaceful Dove
Symbolizes Serenity

Pure and gentle, a soft white grace
Embodiment of peace in every place
Amid life's chaos, a calm profound
Cooing softly, a tranquil sound
Envisioning worlds without strife
Flying above, a serene life
Universal sign of love and peace
Light bearer, conflicts cease

The Hopeful Swallow Sings of Spring's Return

Herald of spring, wings agile and light
Over meadows you take your flight
Pursuer of dreams across the blue sky
Eagerly dancing where the breezes lie
Flight paths marked by hope's own song
Uplifting spirits, you glide along
Liberator of winter's past, ushering delight

Hummingbird's Happiness

In the garden's heart, a flutter small,
The hummingbird darts, over the wall and all.
Ruby-throated, emerald-winged sprite,
Dancing in the sunlight, a delightful sight.

Zipping here, then darting there,
In the sweetened air, without a care.
Sipping nectar from each bloom,
Its tiny heart goes zoom and zoom.

A burst of joy, so swift and keen,
In flashes of vibrant green.
A living jewel, midst petals bright,
Embodies pure, aerial delight.

Oh, to share in its joyous flight,
A blur of beauty, bold and light.
Each beat a whisper of life's fine thrum,
In the garden's heart, where joy comes from.

The Cheerful Robin Sings at Dawn

Crimson-breasted harbinger of day
Heartily singing the chill away
Enthusiastic in the morning light
Evoking joy with pure delight
Resonating warmth through song
Friend to all as days grow long
Uplifting with each note played
Luminous, never dismayed

The Enthusiastic Squirrel Dashes Through the Trees

Energetic leaps from branch to branch
Never tiring, a constant dance
Tiny heart pounding with zest
Harvesting acorns, never at rest
Unabated energy, always in motion
Scurrying about with pure devotion
Inquisitive eyes, a fluffy tail
Adventurous spirit that never fails
Sprightly forager, joyfully wild
Tree-bound acrobat, nature's child
Inspiring all with boundless glee
Cheerful and bustling as can be

The Successful Lion Rules the Savanna

Sovereign of the plains, a majestic sight
Unchallenged power in the golden light
Commanding presence, fearsome and grand
Courageous heart, ruling the land
Essence of strength, pride's royal head
Silent roars that fill the air with dread
Stately mane, a crown of wild gold
Fierce in pursuit, bold and bold
Undisputed king, nature's own law
Leader by nature, with awe we draw
Living legend, wild and free

Fierce Hearts, Tender Shadows

In the jungle's heart, under moon's glow,
A tiger and tigress, love's fierce show.
To the world, their roars spread fear,
But together, they hold each other dear.

His stripes, her grace, through shadows weave,
In whispered love, they both believe.
Fearless alone, but together true,
In each other's gaze, the world anew.

By starlight, their fierce love is seen,
In the quiet night, they reign supreme.
The world may fear their mighty roar,
Yet for each other, their hearts soar.

The Loving Swan Glides on the Lake

Luminous presence in twilight's embrace
Over serene waters, a ballet of grace
Vows of fidelity, together they stay
In mirrored lakes where they play
Neck curved gently, a heart's shape
Graceful partners in feathered drape

Portrait in Ice

Patiently waiting on icy shores,
Each one stands, endures the fierce cold.
Night falls as they huddle for warmth,
Gentle creatures in stark, white worlds.
Under southern stars, they nest,
Intricate dances for beauty, they perform.
Never wavering, guardians of the snow.

The Serene Panda Rests Among Bamboo

Shadowed groves, a peaceful retreat
Eating bamboo, a tranquil feat
Resting calmly under leafy canopies
Enigmatic giant, at ease in the breeze
Nurturing quiet, a gentle soul
Enveloped in green, playing its role

The Mind's Quiet Landscape

Amid the hustle of the bustling day,
Where thoughts like wild rivers sway,
There lies a secret, quiet place,
Crafted by the mind's gentle embrace.

A mountain stands, noble and high,
In photographs, under the sky,
Yet, it's not the image that calms the soul,
But the feeling it stirs, making us whole.

Serenity is not just a sight to behold,
But a state of mind, precious and bold.
In the heart's deep chambers, quietly kept,
Lies the peace where our elation has slept.

What use are pictures if the heart is blind,
To the beauty and peace they're meant to find?
It's the inner stillness that we must seek,
In every moment, every day of the week.

For serenity is a creation of our own,
A seed from the calmness we have sown,
A breath of air, a touch of grace,
A quiet landscape, our mental space.

So gaze upon those mountains high,
Or close your eyes and simply sigh,
For in your thoughts, peace will come to play,
And in your heart, serenity will stay.

The Vibrant Flamingo Stands in Shallow Waters

Vivid hues of pink and red
In shallow marshes, they tread
Balletic stance, one leg to stand
Reflections ripple over sand
Array of colors, strikingly bold
Noble creature, beauty untold
Tropical vision, elegantly composed

The Thriving Beaver Builds at the River

Timber feller, architect fine
Home builder by the waterline
Rippling streams, a dam takes shape
Industrious worker, no escape
Vital to the wetland's health
Ingenious builder, by stealth
Nature's engineer, tail flat
Guardian of the water habitat

A Narwhal's Tale

In the icy seas so far and wide,
A narwhal swims with unique pride.
His spiral horn, a sight to see,
A jousting lance from deep blue sea.

Tales spun of unicorns of old,
In Arctic waters, bold and cold.
This tusk, a tooth so rare and fine,
Through polar dances, it does shine.

Why does the narwhal bear this spear?
A mystery that draws us near.
Is it a wand, or just for show,
Or secrets that the ocean knows?

He twirls it through the icy flow,
A magical staff, it seems to glow.
A tool to stir the sea's deep song,
In waters where the whales belong.

The narwhal's horn, a marvel true,
In the ocean's vast, a wondrous hue.
So let's salute this spirited horn,
A unicorn's gift, sea-born and worn.

The Blissful Sheep Grazes in the Meadow

Beneath blue skies, woolly herds roam
Leisurely grazing, in fields their home
Idyllic scenes, soft and serene
Soft bleats echo, a pastoral scene
Simple joys of nature's embrace
Flock together, a gentle pace
Untroubled life, peaceful and sweet
Lambs at play, their joy complete

The Brilliant Owl Observes the Night

Beneath the moon, keen eyes watch
Ruler of twilight, shadows detach
In silent flight, wings unfold
Lore of wisdom, age-old told
Looking through darkness, sight so keen
Illuminating secrets, rarely seen
Ancient guardian, perched so high
Nocturnal hunter, the moon's ally
Teacher of mystery, in the night sky

Warmth beyond measure

In gentle touch, affection speaks,
Soft as the blush on quiet cheeks.
It's in the hug that lingers long,
In tender words that right the wrong.

A smile that lights the darkest day,
A hand that guides when lost the way.
Its warmth that seeps into the bones,
Filling spaces, healing unknowns.

Like sunlight through the morning mist,
Affection's touch cannot be missed.
It wraps around, a cozy shawl,
Lifting up, whenever we fall.

In every act, both big and small,
Affection's grace stands tall.

It's love's soft whisper, pure and true,
In everything we say and do.

So let us cherish this sweet gift,
Allowing hearts and souls to lift.
For with affection, gently given,
We make our lives a heaven riven.

The Sparkling Hummingbird Dances Between Flowers

Sunlit jewels darting in the air
Petite and vibrant, beyond compare
Aerial acrobat, a blur of speed
Radiance unmatched, in every deed
Kaleidoscope of colors bright
Light as air, pure delight
In gardens blooming, they play their part
Nectar collector, art in heart
Gleaming tiny, life's vibrant spark

The Upbeat Chipmunk Collects with Cheer

Uplifted spirit, quick and clear
Pocketing nuts for the winter near
Bustling through the underbrush
Energetic scamper, a sudden rush
Alive with joy, a tireless quest
Tiny forager, never at rest

A Cat's "Purr"suit

Cat in the world looks for a bird,
A silent tale, rarely heard.
Through rustling leaves and whispering trees,
The cat moves with expert ease.

Eyes alight with keen intent,
On feathered whispers, its mind is bent.
The dance of chase, of hide and seek,
In every shadow, it does peek.

With each soft step, the thrill grows,
In the cat's heart, excitement flows.
A world alive with endless play,
Each moment rich, night and day.

Yet beyond the hunt, there's more to see,
In the cat's gaze, curiosity.
Not just a bird, but life's grand stage,
Explored anew at every age.

The Satisfied Cat Basks in the Sun

Serenely lying, day's work done
Aloof in repose, under the sun
Tail curled neatly, eyes half shut
In every corner, a favorite spot
Soft purring, a contented song
Feline grace, where shadows throng
Independent life, with tranquil charm
Elegant poise, no need for alarm
Dreaming deeply, peace has spun

The Fortunate Rabbit Hops Along

Frolicking freely in fields so wide
Opportunities abound on every side
Ready to spring, at any hint
Thriving in meadows, footprints imprint
Unassuming and quick, a flash of white
Nibbling clovers, a gentle bite
Adaptable, surviving every plight
Tales of luck, from dawn to night
Evading shadows with a light-hearted bound

The quiet joy

In the stillness of a simple day,
Where moments softly slip away,
Lies the gentle art of contentment,
A heart at ease, in quiet ascent.

Not in the rush of fleeting wins,
Nor in the grasp of worldly things,
But in the calm of knowing grace,
In the slow, sure pace of life's embrace.

The laughter shared in dimming light,
The stars above, cool and bright,
In these small joys, true peace is found,
Where life's simple pleasures abound.

A cup of tea, a book unread,
Soft pillows piled upon the bed,
A garden walk, a silent thought,
In such small things, contentment's caught.

It whispers not of more or less,
But loves the current state's caress,
For happiness, in purest form,
Is feeling whole, amidst the storm.

So treasure each uncounted breath,
The quiet life, the silent wealth,
For in contentment's gentle hold,
Lies a story most beautifully told.

The Delightful Parrot Chats Vividly

Dazzling feathers of vibrant hues
Eloquent speaker of amusing news
Lively companion, full of jest
Imitating sounds, a vocal fest
Gregarious nature, sociable friend
Humorous chatter, on trends it'll blend
Tropical colors, a vivid blend
Flitting around, joy without end
Uplifting spirits, with every sound
Laughs abound, where parrots are found

The Energetic Cheetah Runs Across the Savannah

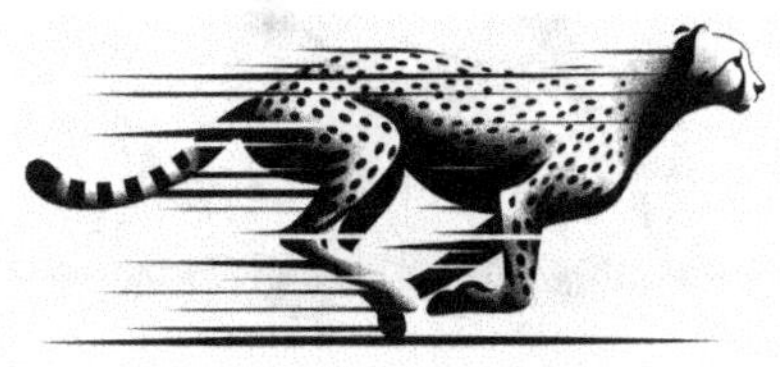

Embodiment of speed, sleek and lean
Nature's racer, barely seen
Elegant stride, a breathtaking rush
Racing heartbeats, the world a hush
Graceful in pursuit, power unleashed
Exquisite runner, from constraints released
Territory vast, chasing the breeze
Incredible agility with the greatest of ease
Commanding presence, fearlessly keen

A Fun squad on hooves

Horses are a fun squad, galloping with glee,
In the meadow's vast embrace, wild and free.
Their hooves beat a rhythm on the soft, green
ground,
A thunder of joy, a magical sound.

Manes flowing like rivers, tails high in the air,
They play in the sunshine, without a care.
Racing the wind, they chase and they dart,
Each burst of their laughter, a work of art.

They toss their heads, and snort, and neigh,
Inviting all who watch to come and play.
In fields of gold, under skies so wide,
They show us how to toss our worries aside.

So come join the fun, feel the grass beneath,
Where the horses run, and take a gentle leap.
For in their company, you'll find it true:
Life's a ride, enjoy the view!

The Positive Meerkat Stands Watch

Perched on hind legs, alert and bright
Observing the lands from morning till night
Social and lively, in groups they thrive
Interacting, they keep the spirit alive
Teamwork in essence, a colony's strength
Insightful watchers, going to great length
Vigilant always, on duty with zest
Each one ready, passing the test

The Flourishing Deer Roams the Forest

Forest dweller, graceful and mild
Loping through woods, nature's child
On velvet hooves, a silent tread
Unseen and heard, where few are led
Regal antlers, crown of the glade
In dappled sunlight, through leaves they wade
Stately presence, a gentle gaze
Harmony found, in forested maze
In nature's bounty, it finds its peace
Nurtured by earth, its grace won't cease
Growing amidst the trees so tall

Compassion's Compass

In the weave of the world's wide web,
Where humanity's threads ebb and flow,
Lies the gentle touch of compassion,
A soft light set to warmly glow.

It's the hand that reaches in the dark,
Finding another's in need of a spark,
The quiet presence beside a bed,
Where words of comfort are softly said.

Compassion dances in a nurse's stride,
In the patience of a teacher's pride,
In the open doors on a cold night,
Where the lost can find some respite.

It lives in the meal shared with the poor,
In the listening ear offered to assure,
In every action, small or grand,
Where kindness moves the heart to stand.

This virtue is not a distant star,
But a close beacon, no matter how far.
It asks for nothing but to give,
And in its giving, teaches us to live.

For in the end, what will remain,
Is not the wealth or the worldly gain,
But the compass of compassion we chose to deploy,
In every act of hope and joy.

So let us weave this thread with care,
Through every fabric of despair,
For in the weave of the human heart,
Compassion is the truest art.

The Creative Spider Weaves Intricate Webs

Crafter of silk, delicate and fine
Radiating lines, design divine
Each thread a masterpiece, skillfully spun
Artist at heart, under the moon and sun
Trapped dew glistens, a morning's lace
Intricate patterns, each with its place
Virtuoso of webs, a silent craft
Enigmatic presence, on air drafts

The Charming Fox Slips Through the Woods

Cunning and sly, a shadow in the night
Hunting quietly, kept out of sight
Adaptable spirit, survivor so keen
Red coat aglow, in places unseen
Mischievous grin, intelligence spark
In wooded realms, it makes its mark
Nimble and quick, a ghostly flame
Grace in each movement, wild and untame

In the grip of Awe

In the hush of the ancient woods,
Where whispers tell of might and moods,
A breath of awe fills the soul's own crease,
In reverence, all noises cease.

Across the canyon's vast embrace,
Under stars that time cannot erase,
The heart stumbles, the mind does pause,
Lost in the wonder of nature's laws.

When a child's laughter fills the air,
Or when love's depth is laid bare,
In these moments, small yet grand,
Awe grips gently by the hand.

It's the ocean's roar on a stormy night,
A comet streaking in celestial flight,
The intricate dance of a fluttering leaf,
In each, awe carves its silent relief.

To stand beneath a sky so wide,
Where dreams dare not hide but collide,
Is to feel the universe expand,
Inside the palm of your trembling hand.

Awe is not just a moment caught,
But a lesson in every thought,
A reminder of how small we are,
Adrift beneath the infinite star.

So let awe in, let it teach,
Let it reach the depths we beseech,
For in that grip, life grows tall,
In awe, we find the greatest call.

The Amiable Golden Retriever Brings Happiness

Affectionate soul, with a heart so pure
Merry in spirit, love's allure
In every greeting, joy unfurled
Admired for loyalty, throughout the world
Best friend to all, with a wagging tail
Lively and loving, never to fail
Eager to please, with each command

My pride - My country

In the heart of where the Ganges flows,
Beneath the Himalayan snows,
Stirs the spirit of a land so grand,
Here, in my proud Indian strand.

A country where greatness is the air we breathe,
Where ancient cultures weave and seethe,
A tapestry so rich, vibrant and wise,
Under the vast, embracing skies.

From the green fields of the Punjab plains,
To the rhythmic beats of Kerala's rains,
Each corner tells its own proud tale,
In every city, village, hill, and dale.

We honor nature's mighty hand,
In reverence, beside her we stand.
Living within the means she grants,
In her wisdom, our daily chants.

Here, joy is found in simple things,
In the peace and hope that living brings.
Whether rich or poor, young or old,
In smiles of warmth against the cold.

The colors of Holi paint the air,
Diwali lights our fervent prayer,
In unity, diversity's embrace,
In every heart, a sacred space.

So with each day, my pride grows deep,
For the land where ancient gods still sleep,
For India, with her enduring grace,
In her soil, my soul finds its place.

The Courageous Tiger Stalks the Jungle

Camouflaged stripes, a silent tread
Owns the shadows, nothing to dread
Undaunted hunter, eyes aglow
Ruler of the wild, a fearsome show
Admired for strength, a beast so grand
Grace in every muscle, power in command
Eternal symbol of bravery and might
Optimal predator, king of the night
Unmatched in the art of stealthy roam
Sovereign of the forest, its ancient home

The Admirable Falcon Soars High Above

Ascendant flight, wings spread wide
Dominating the skies, with pride
Master of winds, a sight to behold
Incredible speed, bold and bold
Reigning supreme, a vision in flight
Aloft on high, a glorious sight
Beauty in motion, freely soared
Lord of the air, universally adored
Each dive a spectacle, grace epitomized

In Admiration of..

Within your gaze, I find a fire,
A spark that lifts my spirit higher.
Your deeds, a dance of grace and might,
In admiration's soft, sweet light.

Your words, a weave of wisdom's loom,
In rooms of thought, they brightly bloom.
Each step you take, each path you choose,
Shows the strength that you infuse.

A role model, a beacon bright,
Guiding through the darkest night.
Your influence, like stars spread wide,
In you, great virtues coincide.

Admiration, a quiet glow,
A feeling that does ebb and flow.
Yet in your shadow, I am found,
By your greatness, truly bound.

The Generous Elephant Shares its Wisdom

Gentle giant, a memory vast
Encompassing strength, from ages past
Nurturing kin, with a tender heart
Each step a rumble, a natural art
Respected elder, in herds they bond
Offering protection, a love profound
Unwavering loyalty, a family's core
Sage of the savannah, legends galore

The Invigorated Horse
Gallops Freely

In fields of green, its spirit flies
Nostrils flared, under open skies
Velocity pure, mane in the wind
Impressive in stride, unbridled, unpinned
Gallant in bearing, muscles in play
Orchestra of movements, in graceful ballet
Resilient and strong, a vibrant force
Admired for vigor, the noble horse
Thundering hooves, a rhythmic dance
Emotion in motion, given the chance

A Sonnet to Small Wonders

Upon the ground, the ants in earnest toil,
A kingdom small, beneath the sun's high boil.
In lines they march, a black and bustling flow,
Each grain of sand, a castle's stone to stow.

Above, the bees with busy wings do soar,
From bloom to bloom, their nectar stores
implore.
In golden fields, where wildflowers freely sway,
They dance their paths, through scented
bouquets.

Both ant and bee, in labor and in dance,
Compose the earth's unseen, vital expanse.
One crafts the earth, one skyward tends to roam,
Yet both in nature's tapestry find home.

In this small world, where many eyes may miss,
Lies beauty vast, and simple, buzzing bliss.
So let us learn from these small lives that strive,
For even the tiniest souls vividly thrive.

The Supportive Ant Builds with Teamwork

Small but mighty, a collective force
United in effort, a common course
Power in numbers, an organized line
Perseverance shared, a design divine
Operations complex, each has a role
Relentless in pursuit, a single goal
Together they build, a structure grand
Industry small, yet proudly they stand
Vital to survival, their teamwork shows
Engineers of the earth, in rows they compose

The Healthy Gazelle Leaps Across the Plains

Head held high, agile and sleek
Elegant jumps, a graceful technique
Alive with vigor, a spirit free
Loping through grasslands, wild and breezy
Thriving in herds, a swift escape
Harmony in motion, a perfect shape
Yielding to no predator, a dance of chance

The Optimistic Bluebird Sings of Hope

Open skies above, a melody rings
Perched on high, where it joyfully sings
Tales of happiness, in notes so clear
Inspiring all who are near
Morning's first light, a song of cheer
Infinite joy, year after year
Symphony of optimism, bright and bold
Trilling sweetly, stories told
In every note, a promise held
Celebration of life, beautifully knelled

The Refreshed Otter Plays in the River

Ripples of laughter, water's playmate
Enjoying each splash, a joyful trait
Frolicking freely, in streams so clear
Revelling in rivers, without any fear
Energetic dives, a spectacle to see
Sliding on belly, in pure glee
Happy in habitat, a playful spree
Exuberance in water, carefree and free
Delight in every wave, life's simple cheer

The Enlightened Crow Holds Secrets of the Old

Eerie calls at twilight's close
Navigator of mysteries, it knows
Lore keeper, of the ancient code
Intelligence in each mode
Guardian of truth, in black it's clad
Harbinger of tales, both good and bad
Tracing through the skies, a shadowed guide
Enigmatic life, in plain sight it hides
Night's own sentinel, watchful and wise
Each caw a chapter, in the skies

The Affectionate Koala Clings to Its Tree

Adorable creature, with a gentle grip
Furry body, in a sleepy zip
Fond of eucalyptus, in trees it stays
Embracing branches, in a tranquil haze
Cuddly form, a peaceful sight
Tender and mild, with delight
In leafy homes, a serene embrace
Offspring close, a loving base
Nurturing quiet, a soft-spoken plea
Affection manifests, on the tree

The Content Sloth Hangs Leisurely

Calmly suspended, in a world up high
Observing the world with a sleepy eye
Not hurried or worried, a slow-paced life
Time on its side, free from strife
Each movement deliberate, conserved energy
Nestled among leaves, a living tapestry
Tranquility embodied, in slow motion

The Exuberant Kangaroo Leaps Across the Outback

Expression of joy, boundless and free
Xenial hops, a sight to see
Unique in motion, a powerful spring
Bouncing high, legs that fling
Enthusiastic jumper, across the land
Rapid movements, spectacularly grand
Adapted to roam, in arid scenes
Natural athlete, strong and lean
Thriving down under, where wild spirits meet

Sunrise in the heart

Each morning holds a promise bright,
A canvas bathed in newborn light.
With every sunrise, hope renews,
A day adorned in vibrant hues.

Look to the sky, where dreams take flight,
Above the clouds, beyond the night.
In every heart, optimism sings,
A melody that sprightly springs.

Life's challenges, like mountains high,
Seem smaller under the vast sky.
With faith, each step leads to the crest,
Where views are clear, and souls feel blessed.

The world spins on, with joys untold,
In every story, new and old.
The heart that looks to find the good,
Discovers love where once it stood.

So let us wear this cheerful crest,
A badge of hope upon our breast.
For with optimism in our sight,
Each day unfolds with new delight.

The Luminous Firefly Glows in the Dark

Light bearer in twilight's park
Under night's canopy, a tiny spark
Mystical dancer, a glowing dart
Illuminating darkness, art of the heart
Nocturnal beacon, softly it glows
Orchestra of lights, a show it bestows
Unseen during the day, in shadows it hides
Shining come dusk, where magic resides

The Empowered Gorilla Stands Mighty in the Forest

Eminent figure, robust and grand
Majestic in stature, on forest land
Power embodied, in each mighty hand
Overlord of the jungle, its command
Wisdom in eyes, an ancient soul
Enforcer of peace, in control
Respectful of kin, a protective role
Enduring strength, an imposing patrol
Dignified presence, nature's own

The Harmonious Whale Sings in the Ocean Depths

Hulking yet gentle, giants of the sea
Abyssal melodies, sung so free
Resonating through waters, deep and vast
Majestic creatures, from ages past
Oceans their stage, a symphonic play
Navigating currents, in a ballet
In harmony with the marine throng
Orchestral giants, with a song so long
Underwater concert, a peaceful lull
Sovereigns of the deep, wonderfully full

A mother's empathy

In the soft folds of a mother's embrace,
Lies the boundless depth of grace.
Her eyes, a mirror to our own,
Reflect the feelings we have shown.

With every tear that we may shed,
She feels the weight in her own stead.
Her heart, a beacon in the night,
Guides us through with gentle light.

She listens to the silent words,
The ones we speak without sound.
Understanding without having to ask,
In her empathy, we safely bask.

She teaches us to see beyond
Our own needs, to the bond

That links all hearts in subtle ways,
Through her example, we learn grace.

Empathy, her gift, she shares,
With every child, she tenderly bears.
In her care, we learn to give,
And in her strength, we learn to live.

For in a mother's empathy,
There's a quiet, vast infinity.
A love that transcends, pure and deep,
In her arms, safe secrets keep.

The Genuine Orangutan Contemplates in the Rainforest

Gracious in demeanor, wise old face
Each movement deliberate, filled with grace
Natural thinker, deep in thought
Understanding the world, without being taught
In treetop homes, a life aloft
Noble guardian, soft and soft
Embodying calm, serene and peaceful

The Friendly Labrador Welcomes Everyone

Faithful companion, ever so sweet
Reliable friend, always a treat
In every greeting, enthusiasm meets
Eager to please, with happy feet
Never a dull moment, with tail in wag
Delight in company, never a lag
Loving to all, a heart so big
Yearning for cuddles, that's the gig

Hope in the Whisper of Wings

In the garden of both everything and naught,
Where the soul's deepest yearnings are quietly
sought,
There blooms a calla lily, stark against the grey,
A symbol of change at the break of day.

Amidst everything, this vast expanse of same,
Where echoes of sameness whisper my name,
A butterfly flutters, fragile and light,
Carrying hopes of a joyful flight.

Though life sometimes feels like a repeating
stage,
Each moment locked inside a gilded cage,
The flutter of wings, the bloom's gentle sway,
Speaks of change that might come our way.

A hope for change is the spice of life,
Cutting through the mundane like a knife.
It's not in the grand, but in the small,
That hope finds its foothold, standing tall.

The lily shifts, the butterfly soars,
Above the tedium that life sometimes pours.
In their dance, there's a promise made:
With hope, the colors of life will never fade.

So let the calla lily rise, let the butterfly roam,
In their change, let our spirits find a home,
For even in a world where everything's the
same,
The hope for change ignites an enduring flame.

The Pleasant Butterfly Flutters in the Garden

Painted wings, delicate and light
Lilting through gardens, a joyful sight
Each color a brushstroke from nature's hand
Adorning flowers, where it might land
Symbol of transformation, beauty's grace
Airy dance, from place to place
Nectar seeker, gentle and mild
Tiny wanderer, nature's child

The Wondrous Narwhal Swims in Arctic Waters

Whimsical creature, unicorn of the sea
Oceanic mystery, wild and free
Northern waters, its icy realm
Diving deep, a tapered helm
Remote and elusive, a sight so rare
Outlandish tusk, beyond compare
Under polar lights, it swims with ease
Surreal presence, in freezing seas

The Productive Honeybee Pollinates the Fields

Profound worker, tireless and small
Regiments of flight, answering nature's call
Organized colonies, a hive's might
Diligent in duty, from dawn till night
Unwavering in their task, to flowers they cling
Creating sweetness, a golden offering
Together they labor, a communal feat
In gardens and meadows, their buzz so sweet
Vital to life, a role so key
Ecosystem's ally, the humble bee

In the wake of the Shark

Beneath the surface, vast and wide,
A sleek form cuts the ocean tide.
A shark, in its relentless quest,
Embodies strength at nature's behest.

With focused gaze and fluid grace,
It conquers the sea's deep embrace.
A hunter honed by time's own hand,
Surviving where others barely stand.

Its path is one of silent will,
In the deep, where waters chill.
Each fin stroke more than mere survival,
A lesson in life's fierce revival.

Admire the shark, its steadfast heart,
From ancient seas, a living art.
Let its spirit your courage spark,
To chase your dreams through light and dark.

The Magical Unicorn Gallops in Mystical Lands

Mythic vision, a creature of lore
Aloft on hooves, through forests it tore
Glimmering mane, a spectral glow
Imagination's seed, in hearts it sow
Celestial being, pure and fair
Ancient symbol of magic, rare
Legendary grace, in dreams it stands

The Passionate Wolf Howls Beneath the Moon

Pack leader, a silhouette against the sky
Ancient caller, a mournful cry
Spirit of the wild, fierce and raw
Stalking the woods, by nature's law
Instinctive hunter, eyes agleam
Ominous presence, in twilight's beam
Noble beast, survival's song
Alpha of the pack, where wolves belong
Territorial pride, fiercely held
Echoing howls, passionately swelled

The Warm Sheep Grazes Under the Sun

Woolly coats under golden rays
Amidst the fields, where they graze
Relaxed and docile, a gentle throng
Meandering quietly, all day long

The Jubilant Macaw
Squawks from the Treetops

Joyous colors flash through leaves
Uplifting calls, the forest heaves
Brilliant plumage, an echo loud
In tropical canopies, proudly avowed
Lively spirit, vibrant and keen
Aerial artist, a sight serene
Nature's own carnival, bright and clear

www.ingramcontent.com/pod-product-compliance
Lightning Source LLC
LaVergne TN
LVHW020055210726
843507LV00016B/2549